Contents

Basic equipment

1 Cake smoothers
2 Ribbon
3 Parchment piping bag
4 Piping tubes/nozzles/tips
5 Cake box
6 Turntable
7 Water bottle and brush
8 Cake tins
9 Foam/sponge pad
10 Sable paintbrushes/flat dusting brush
11 Wire cutters
12 Non-stick rolling pins
13 Cake dowels
14 Cake boards
15 Sugarcraft wires
16 Small non-stick board
17 Large non-stick board
18 Knives - serrated, sharp, palette and craft

Specialist equipment and consumables

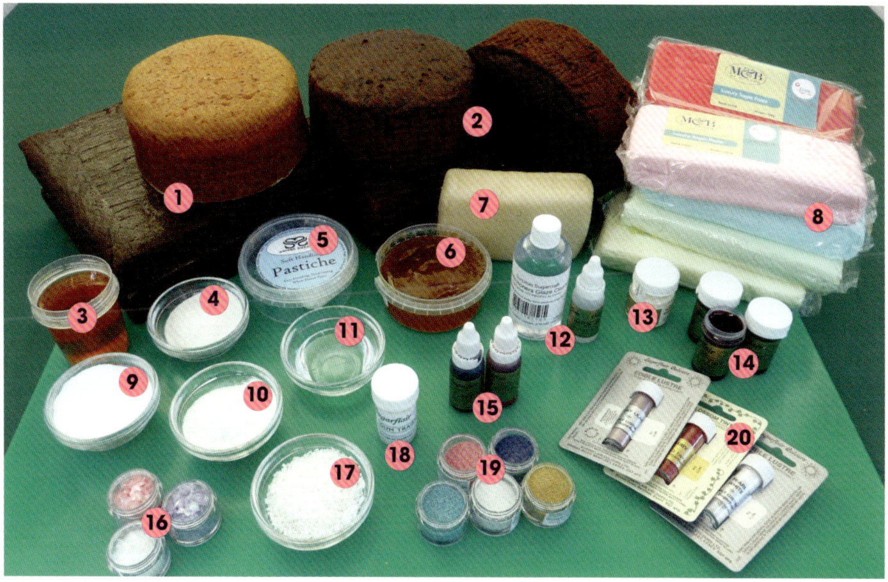

1 Sponge cake
2 Rich fruit cake
3 Confectioners varnish /glaze
4 Tylose powder
5 Flower paste
6 Apricot glaze
7 Marzipan
8 Sugarpaste
9 Icing sugar
10 Egg albumen – Meri-White
11 Liquid glucose
12 Isopropyl alcohol/rejuvenator fluid/dipping solution
13 Gildesol
14 Paste food colour
15 Liquid food colour
16 Magic Sparkles
17 Desiccated coconut
18 Gum tragacanth (GT)
19 Edible glitter
20 Blossom tint/dusting powder

1 Bead cutter/maker
2 Multi-ribbon cutter
3 Letter cutters
4 Sugar shaper/clay gun
5 Size guide
6 6-petalled daisy cutters
7 Crimpers
8 Bow cutter
9 Holly cutters
10 Robin cutters
11 Bell cutters
12 Circle cutters
13 Blossom cutters
14 Flower picks
15 Non-stick icing sheet
16 Butterfly cutters
17 Design wheeler
18 Bone/dogbone tool
19 Quilting tool/mini stitch wheel/dresden tool
20 Scriber/needle tool
21 Calyx cutters

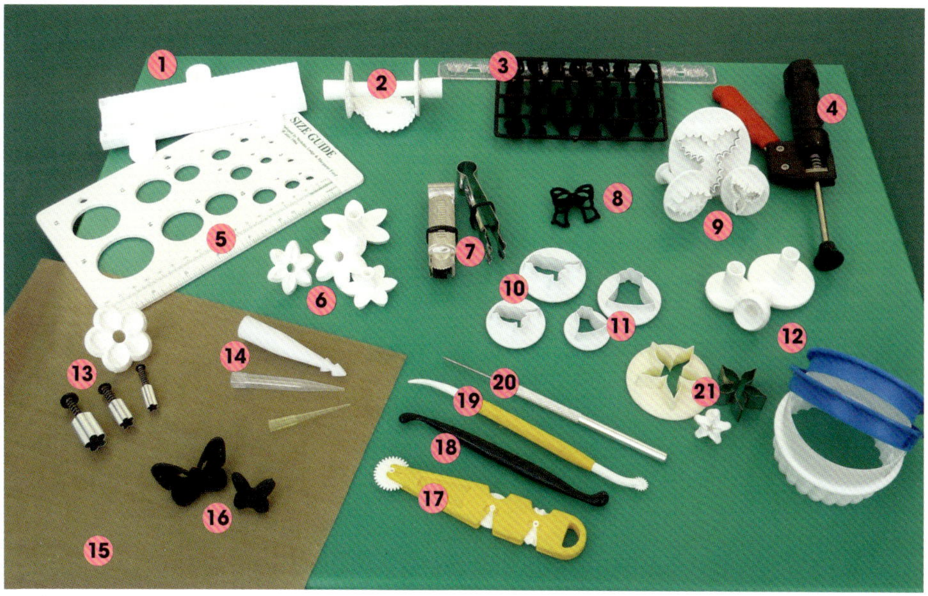

Rich fruit cake recipe chart

Ingredients	15cm (6in) round 13cm (5in) square	18cm (7in) round 15cm (6in) square	20cm (8in) round 18cm (7in) square	23cm (9in) round 20cm (8in) square	25cm (10in) round 23cm (9in) square
Sultanas	100g (4oz)	175g (6oz)	225g (8oz)	275g (10oz)	400g (14oz)
Raisins	100g (4oz)	175g (6oz)	225g (8oz)	275g (10oz)	400g (14oz)
Currants	150g (5oz)	200g (7oz)	250g (9oz)	325g (12oz)	450g (1lb)
Mixed peel	40g (1½oz)	50g (2oz)	75g (3oz)	100g (4oz)	150g (5oz)
Glacé cherries	50g (2oz)	75g (3oz)	100g (4oz)	175g (6oz)	200g (7oz)
Orange juice/sherry	125ml (4fl oz)	150ml (5fl oz)	175ml (6fl oz)	225ml (8fl oz)	325ml (12fl oz)
Almonds, chopped	15g (½oz)	25g (1oz)	25g (1oz)	50g (2oz)	75g (3oz)
Lemon grated rind	½	½	1	1	1
Black treacle	1 dessertspoon	1 dessertspoon	1 tablespoon	1 tablespoon	1½ tablespoon
Butter/margarine	100g (4oz)	175g (6oz)	225g (8oz)	275g (10oz)	400g (14oz)
Brown sugar	100g (4oz)	175g (6oz)	225g (8oz)	275g (10oz)	400g (14oz)
Eggs, medium	2	3	4	5	7
Plain flour	100g (4oz)	175g (6oz)	225g (8oz)	275g (10oz)	400g (14oz)
Self-raising flour	25g (1oz)	50g (2oz)	75g (3oz)	100g (4oz)	150g (5oz)
Cinnamon	¼ teaspoon	½ teaspoon	1 level teaspoon	1 level teaspoon	1¼ teaspoon
Mixed spice	¼ teaspoon	½ teaspoon	1 level teaspoon	1 level teaspoon	1¼ teaspoon
Nutmeg	¼ teaspoon	½ teaspoon	½ teaspoon	½ teaspoon	1 teaspoon
Salt	pinch	¼ teaspoon	¼ teaspoon	½ teaspoon	½ teaspoon
Baking time	2 hours	3 hours	3½ hours	3½ - 4 hours	4½ - 5 hours

Method

1. Soak the fruit in the orange juice/sherry for 24 hours, turning it once or twice.
2. Grease and line the cake tin. Set oven to Gas 7/220°C/425°F.
3. Sieve the flour with the spices and salt. Grate the lemon rind.
4. Beat the butter/margarine and sugar until creamy and light, and then add the lemon rind and black treacle.
5. Beat the eggs together and gradually whisk them into the mixture a little at a time with two/three tablespoons of flour.
6. Fold in the remaining flour with the fruit and nuts. Check the consistency, it should drop easily from the spoon. If it doesn't, add a little milk.
7. Put the mixture into the lined tin and make a slight hollow in the centre with a wooden spoon dipped in water.
8. Place in the oven and turn the temperature down to Gas 1/140°C/275°F. For a fan oven refer to the manufacturers instructions.
9. The cake is done when it is a good brown colour and a skewer inserted comes out clean. If you listen to the cake you should not hear it bubbling.
10. Once the cake is cold, keep the paper on and brush brandy, rum or sherry on the cake surface. Cover with paper and wrap in foil.

Tips

- Use a mixture of margarine and butter. The margarine gives a better aeration to the cake and the butter gives a good flavour.
- A 50:50 mixture of medium/dry sherry and orange juice gives a good flavour.
- Use the best quality fruit etc. possible to give the best results.
- Ideally store the cake for a month before using.
- Use either imperial or metric measurements not a mixture of both or the recipe balance will be incorrect.

Sponge cake recipe chart

Ingredients	15cm (6in) round 13cm (5in) square	18cm (7in) round 15cm (6in) square	20cm (8in) round 18cm (7in) square	23cm (9in) round 20cm (8in) square	25cm (10in) round 23cm (9in) square
Eggs, medium	2	3	4	5	7
Butter/margarine	100g (4oz)	175g (6oz)	225g (8oz)	275g (10oz)	400g (14oz)
Caster sugar	100g (4oz)	175g (6oz)	225g (8oz)	275g (10oz)	400g (14oz)
Self-raising flour	100g (4oz)	175g (6oz)	225g (8oz)	275g (10oz)	400g (14oz)
Baking Time					
One tin	35 - 45 mins	40 - 45 mins	45 - 50 mins	1 hour	1-1½ hours
Two tins	20 - 25 mins	25 - 30 mins	30 mins	40 mins	45 mins
Butter Icing					
Icing sugar	150g (5oz)	200g (7oz)	250g (9oz)	275g (10oz)	325g (12oz)
Butter/margarine	65g (2½oz)	100g (4oz)	125g (4½oz)	150g (5oz)	175g (6oz)

Method

1. Grease and line the cake tin/s. Heat the oven to Gas 4/180°C/350°F.
2. Beat the fat and sugar together until light in colour and texture.
3. Beat the eggs together then whisk or beat them into the mixture a little at a time with a spoonful of flour.
4. Sieve any remaining flour into the mixture and fold this in with a large metal spoon.
5. The consistency should be soft and drop from the spoon easily when shaken. If it is too stiff add a little milk.
6. Add flavouring of choice and for a plain cake add a few drops of vanilla essence.
7. Place in the tin/s and bake. To test if it is done, insert a skewer in the centre and it should come out clean when removed. You can also press a finger on the cake top and when cooked the sponge will spring back and also have started to shrink away from the tin sides. Turn out and allow to cool.
8. Make the butter icing. Soften the butter to room temperature and gradually beat in the sieved icing sugar and flavouring if used.

Tips

- This recipe can be made as an all-in-one mixture by adding ½ teaspoon of baking powder per 100g (4oz) of flour.
- Have all the ingredients at room temperature before starting to bake.
- For larger cakes it is often more satisfactory to bake two cakes rather than one.
- Once baked the sponge cake can be kept for a week (or well wrapped and frozen).
- Cool the cake and then fill and coat with the butter icing. The cake must be completely cold, otherwise moisture can be trapped inside and encourage mould. Then lightly coat the outside with the remaining icing.
- You can flavour the butter icing with: vanilla, coffee, almond essence. Lemon or orange finely grated zest. Lemon or orange curd. Praline, made from caramelised sugar and crushed nuts. Crushed fruit, spirits or liqueurs. Chocolate (melt and use at a ratio of 50g (2oz) per 100g (4oz) butter approximately).
- Store in a cool place.
- Baking times are approximate.

Marzipan and sugarpaste quantities

Ingredients	15cm (6in) round 13cm (5in) square	18cm (7in) round 15cm (6in) square	20cm (8in) round 18cm (7in) square	23cm (9in) round 20cm (8in) square	25cm (10in) round 23cm (9in) square
Marzipan	500g (1lb 1oz)	750g (1lb 10oz)	875g (2lb)	1kg (2lb 4oz)	1.25kg (2lb 12oz)
Sugarpaste	625g (1lb 6oz)	875g (2lb)	1kg (2lb 4oz)	1.25kg (2lb 12oz)	1.5kg (3lb 5oz)

Basic recipes - Royal icing

Ingredients

Icing sugar (sieved)	1.75k (3½lb)
Water	315ml (½pt)
Albumen powder	45g (1½oz)

Method

1 Place the mixing bowl on your scales and pour in the albumen solution through a sieve. This will avoid any lumps in the mixture and ensure the correct amount. If you add the mixture without weighing there will be too much moisture.

2 Sieve the icing sugar into the bowl. Use the mixer paddle to stir the ingredients together before beating on the slowest speed. Times will vary depending on the speed of your mixer but as a rough guide it takes between 4-6 minutes to reach soft peak consistency.

3 Keep the icing covered with a slightly damp cloth whilst you are working with it and keep checking that it has not dried out.

4 To store, place the icing in a bowl with a tight lid. Cover the surface with clingfilm and press it down for extra protection.

OR

Icing sugar	500g (1lb)
Water	90ml (6 tablespoon)
Albumen powder	15g (1 tablespoon)

Egg White (albumen) – powdered versions are recommended, either pure dried albumen (e.g. Renwhite) or a substitute (e.g. Meri-white). As well as complying with food safety regulations these give a consistent result, which is difficult with fresh egg white due to variations in size and water content. There is a difference in colour and when mixed with water, the substitute powder dissolves almost immediately. Pure albumen forms a sticky mass, and needs to be soaked for at least an hour to dissolve, but it is far stronger for delicate work.

Soft Peak – is used for coating, lettering, bulbs and line piping. To test, press the flat of the blade of a palette knife into the icing, and pull into a peak. This should stand up easily and the tip bend slightly with the softness.

Full Peak – is required when using star and rope tubes, piped flowers or anything which requires good definition when piping. To make this consistency, return the icing to the mixer and continue to beat until the peak stands rigid. Between 2-4 minutes extra.

Mexican paste

Icing sugar	250g (8oz)
Gum Tragacanth	15ml (3 teaspoon)
Liquid glucose	5ml (1 teaspoon)
Water	30ml (6 teaspoon)

Method

1 Sieve the icing sugar and gum tragacanth together into a bowl.

2 Add the water and the liquid glucose and bind the mixture together.

3 Turn on to a board dusted with icing sugar and knead until smooth.

4 Store in a polythene bag inside a sealed container.

Note: Occasionally extra water may be necessary, add this at the kneading stage.

Sugar glue

Tylopur (Tylose Powder)
Water
Small water bottle and brush

Method

1 Nearly fill the bottle with water.

2 Dip a teaspoon handle end into Tylopur (Tylose Powder) and add this amount to the bottle. Replace the cap and shake well. The mixture will be lumpy.

3 Leave a while and shake the bottle again, repeat until the powder has mixed into the water to produce a 'wallpaper paste' like consistency.

Modelling paste

Mix sugarpaste and flower or mexican paste 50:50 to give a paste that is firmer than sugarpaste on its own and still tastes good.

Alternatively you can make modelling paste by adding 1 teaspoon of gum tragacanth or CMC to 500g/1lb of sugarpaste and knead it well in. Store the paste in a polythene bag to keep the air out.

Apricot glaze

This can be bought ready-made but you can also make it by placing 100g (4oz) cheap apricot jam (no large pieces of fruit) into a pan with 2 tablespoons water. Heat gently until the jam softens then bring to the boil and simmer for 1 minute. Sieve and use hot.

How to coat a cake

1 Measure the cake with a tape measure across the top and down both sides and add 2.5cm (1in) to this measurement. Fill any indentations in the cake with marzipan. If the surface of the cake is uneven, brush the shoulder with glaze and add a fat sausage of marzipan before turning the cake over so that what was the base now becomes the cake top. Brush the top and sides of the cake with boiled apricot glaze.

2 Lightly dust the work surface with icing sugar and roll out the marzipan to the measurement you made earlier. You can use spacers so the marzipan is an even thickness. Lift the marzipan onto a rolling pin or support it on both arms and unroll over the surface of the cake. Lift the paste as you mould it to the contour of the cake. Smooth with a cake smoother and trim away the surplus marzipan.

3 Gently work the sugarpaste for the covering, to give a soft pliable paste. Try not to knead too vigorously as this will incorporate air bubbles and these will show in the final finish. Roll out the sugarpaste (between spacers if you have these) and then polish the surface with a smoother. Do not get any icing sugar on the top surface of the paste, be distracted or work in a draft as this will cause crazing on the surface.

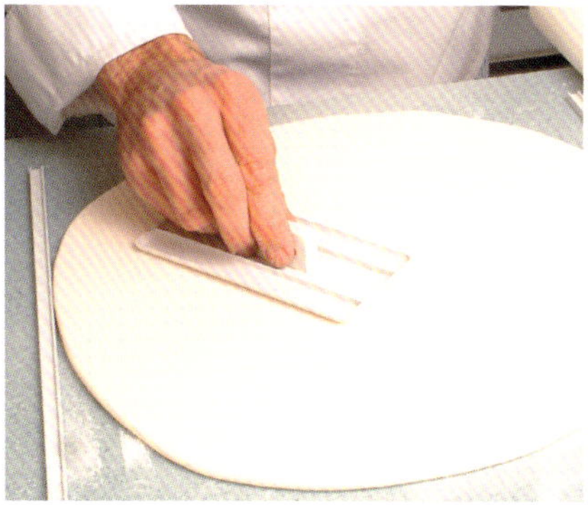

4 Place the cake on the cake board. Brush the marzipan with clear alcohol. Lift the paste onto a rolling pin, and then unroll over the cake. Shape the sugarpaste around the cake and trim away the excess, around the edge of the cake board.

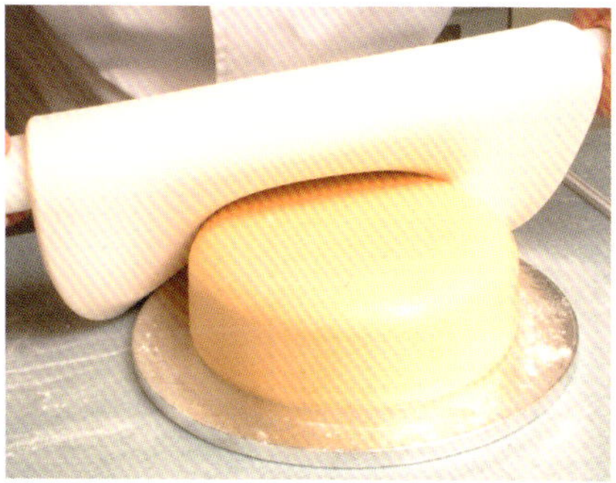

5 Polish the surface of the cake with smoothers. To get a straight side you can use a special angled smoother, which forms a neat covering on the cake and the board in one movement.

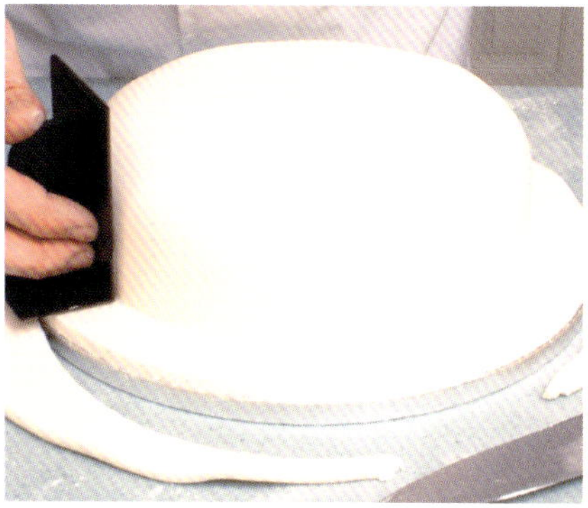

6 Alternatively trim the sugarpaste away around the base of the cake. Place the cake on its board. Moisten the board and roll out a strip of sugarpaste. Lay this around the board and trim at an angle. Smooth over the join and trim the excess away from the board edge.

How to make a piping bag

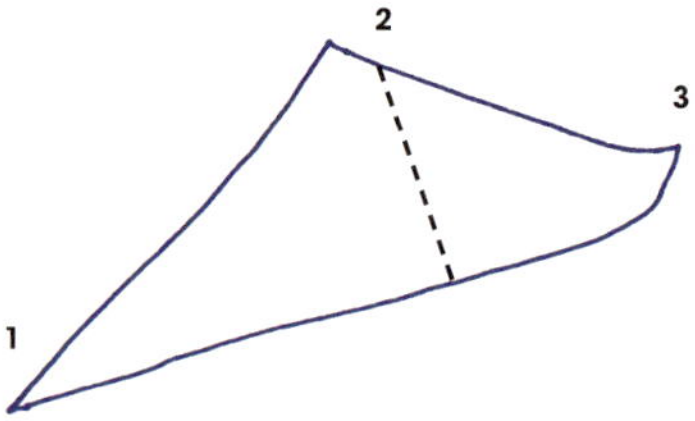

1 Cut baking parchment into triangles as per the template (on page 47). Keep a selection of these triangles ready to make into bags as you need them.

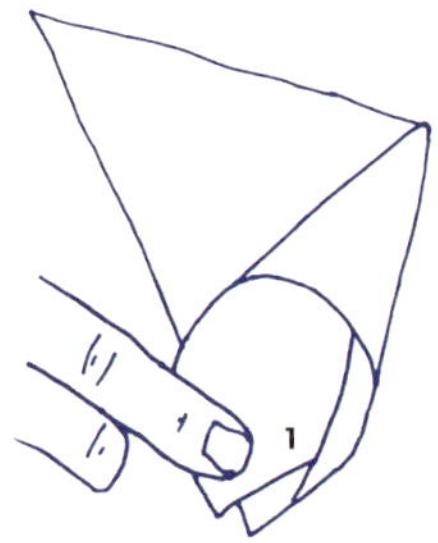

2 Roll corner No. 1 towards line 2.

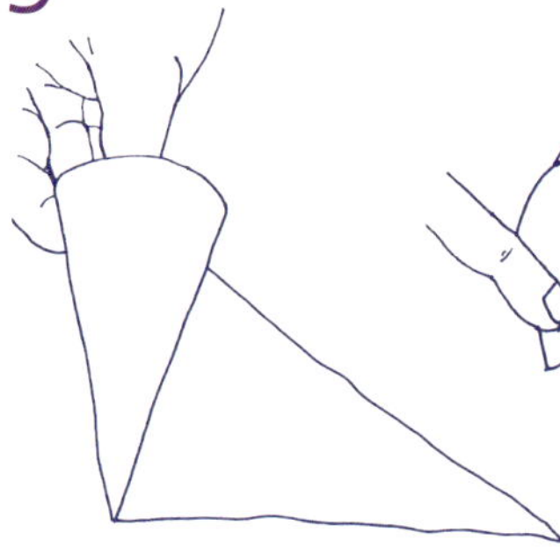

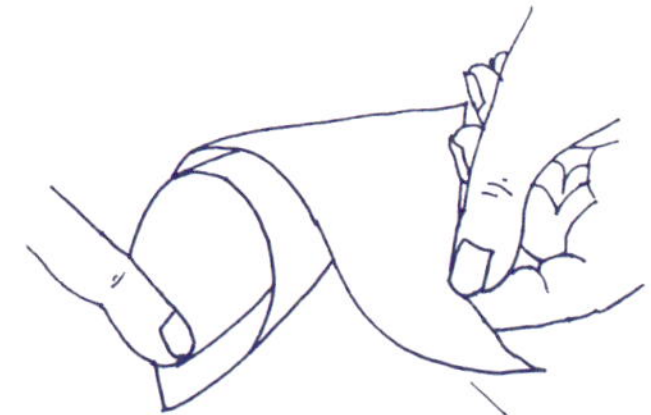

3 Take corner 3 and fold it over the top and around the back of the cone. It is important that the point formed is very sharp, you may need to slide the corners of the triangle up and down until it is tight.

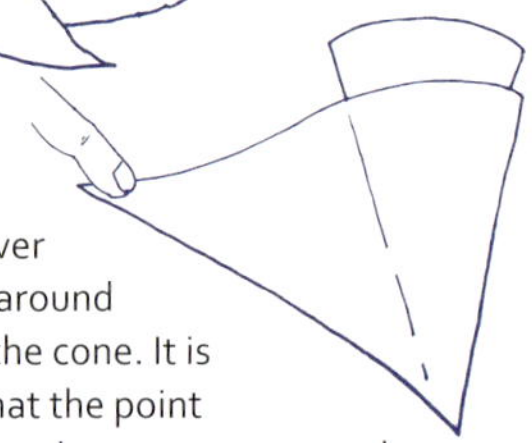

4 Fold the top points over into the cone.

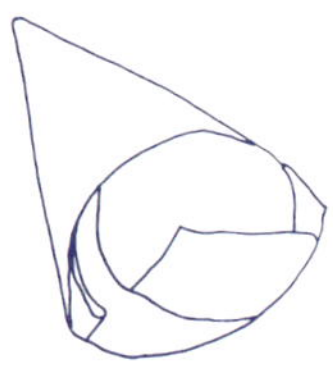

5 Tear or cut two slits about 1cm long and 1cm apart. Fold this piece out over the back of the cone. You should now have a secure cone.

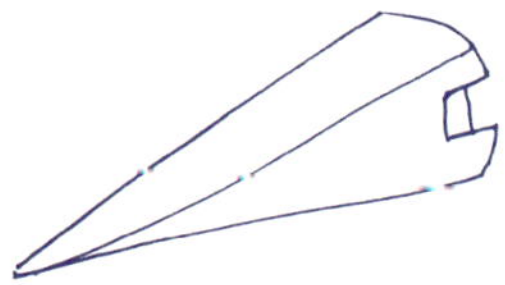

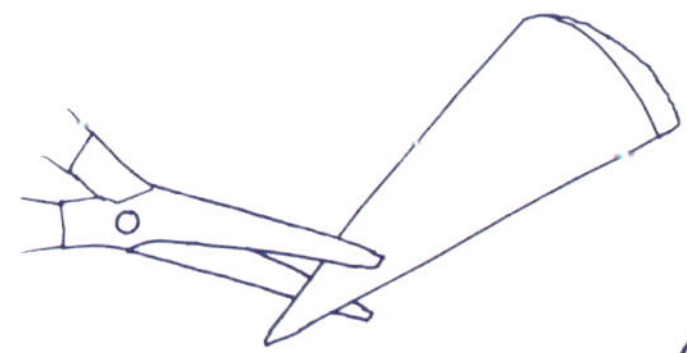

6 Snip a small piece (about 1.5cm) from the tip of the cone and drop in the nozzle.

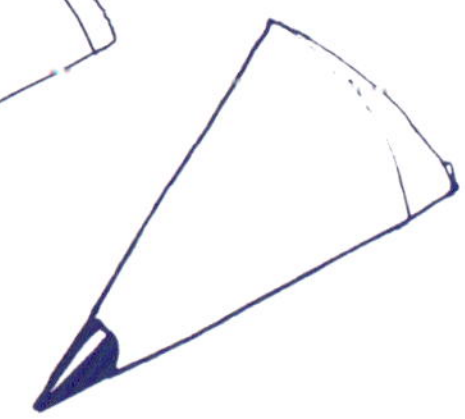

7 Use a palette knife to half fill the cone with icing.

8 Fold over the top of the cone and you are ready to begin piping. Always keep the join in the bag at the back. The join will tighten each time you fold down the top edge.

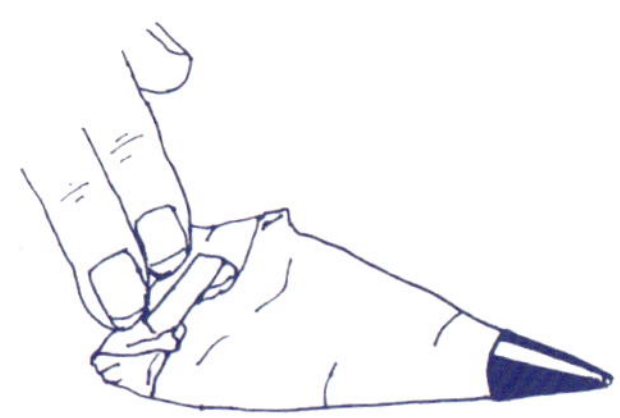

Line piping

Use a plain round writing tube and soft peak icing. Hold the bag in your hand and steady this hand with your other hand. Touch the cake surface with the tube end, keep the bag at an angle of 45° with the other hand. Squeeze the bag steadily until the icing appears. Continue to apply pressure whilst lifting the bag and tube in the direction of the line to be piped. Before reaching the end of the line release the pressure and lower the tube to the cake surface. Pull the bag cleanly away. Wipe the end of the tube with a clean damp cloth. Keep the tip of the tube under a damp cloth when not in use.

To pipe curved lines, touch the cake surface, keeping the tube at 60° and continue to pipe whilst lifting the bag in the direction of the curve. Release the pressure just before the end and lower the tube down to the cake to finish piping.

Shell piping

Use a star or rope tube and firm peak icing. Hold the tube lightly against the surface and push out a well rounded bulb. Release the pressure and pull the tube away towards you to form a short tail. Keep it at the same angle, if you lift the bag upwards it will create a dent in the tail. Start the next bulb just in front of the last tail, so that when you apply pressure the bulb covers the tip of the previous shell. A perfect shell should be rounded and separately defined from its neighbour.

Basic piping techniques

No matter how beautifully decorated a cake is, somehow it seems all that bit more special to have a name or inscription on it or the cake board. Children particularly love anything that is theirs. It takes time and practice to perfect your piped inscriptions but one thing that will make the letters look better is to get them straight (or curved if the design works better this way) and evenly spaced.

Make A Template

There are a few tricks you can use to achieve neat lettering. Make a greaseproof paper template of the cake top (taking into account the rest of the design) and write your letters neatly on this in pencil, then you can rub the marks out and start again until the positioning looks good.

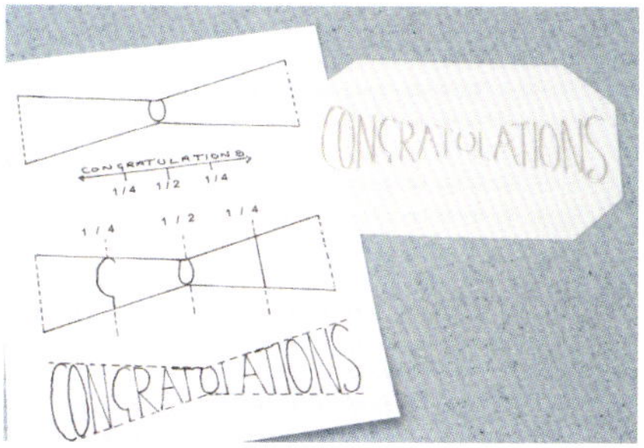

To fit lettering into an unusual shape, first draw out the shape in the size required. Write out the lettering in your own handwriting below this, measure the length and note the centre point. Draw the centre letter and work outwards either side to complete the word. Position the paper on the cake top and scribe the letters on the sugarpaste. This gives you an outline to follow as you pipe.

How To Pipe The Letters

Until you are very confident pipe the letters in the same colour as the cake, then if you make a mistake any removal marks will blend in with the cake coating. You can then 'overpipe' the letters on top in coloured royal icing. The icing will fall easily onto the letter underneath. Use a larger tube for the underneath letters - No. 2 or 1.5 and a smaller tube on top - No. 1.5 or 1. Hold the writing tube vertically and apply pressure without moving the tube. The icing will pipe out in circles. This is the principle you use for piping small curves and circles.

When piping lettering there are two techniques that cause problems, first is letters with small curves. When you reach the point where there is a small curve such as on an 'h', apply extra pressure and the icing will form a curve automatically. Letters with two joins such as 'b' or 'd' are tricky. Remember to release the pressure on the piping tube before you reach the final join and then gently touch it against the line. Alternatively avoid a second join by leaving a gap or curl the end of the piping inwards.

Paste Letters

If you would prefer not to pipe the inscriptions you can create lettering from thinly rolled out flower or mexican paste using tappits, strip cutters, block cutters or individual letter cutters (all types come with their own instructions). The advantage of paste letters is that you can allow them to dry on a piece of sponge before positioning them on the cake. Once in position stick the letters down with sugar glue. A small ruler will help to line the letters up so they are even. You can also make a template for curved or even shapes for where the lettering will follow the curve of a round cake.

Flowers and Fairies

This is a very forgiving design as any parts of the cake coating that are not perfect can be covered with a leaf or two! A simpler design could be made by making a ring of leaves and fairies around the top edge of the cake. A fairy placed on top of a cupcake would make a very special gift for all the party guests.

How to make

1 Level the cake if necessary and slice into two or three layers. Reassemble, sandwiching the layers together with buttercream.

2 With the cake in the centre of the cake board spread a thin coating of buttercream around the sides and top.

3 To cover the cake first dust the work surface with icing sugar. Knead and roll out 500g (1lb 2oz) white sugarpaste. Place over the cake. Smooth the top and sides and trim and neaten the base.

4 To cover the board lightly moisten the exposed cake board around the base of the cake with water.

5 Measure the circumference of the cake and the distance from the edge of the cake to the edge of the board. Thinly roll out the remaining white sugarpaste and cut out a strip slightly wider than needed.

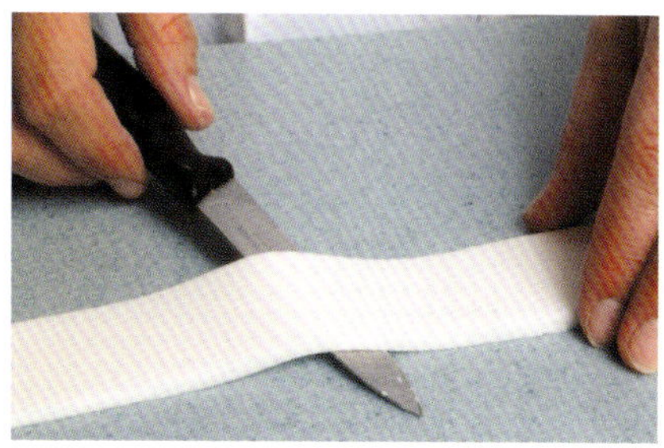

shopping list

- round sponge cake 15cm (6in)
- round cake board 25cm (10in)
- buttercream 500g (1lb)
- sugarpaste 2kg (4lb)
- rice paper 1 - 2 sheets
- blossom cutter
- assorted paste food colours

6 Slide a knife along under the strip to ensure that it is not stuck to the work surface and roll it up like a bandage. Unwind the bandage around the cake board. Neaten the join and trim the edges.

7 Roll out a small piece of the green sugarpaste. Cut out a few very simple leaf shapes. Press in a few veins with the back of a knife and stick onto the cake with dabs of water.

8 Roll out pink sugarpaste and cut out a few flowers with the blossom cutter. Place these amongst the leaves. Cover the cake top and the board. Place a small yellow sugarpaste ball in the centre of each flower.

9 Roll a tiny bit of flesh coloured sugarpaste into a thin sausage. Bend in half and attach to the cake. Make about 20/25 sets of legs.

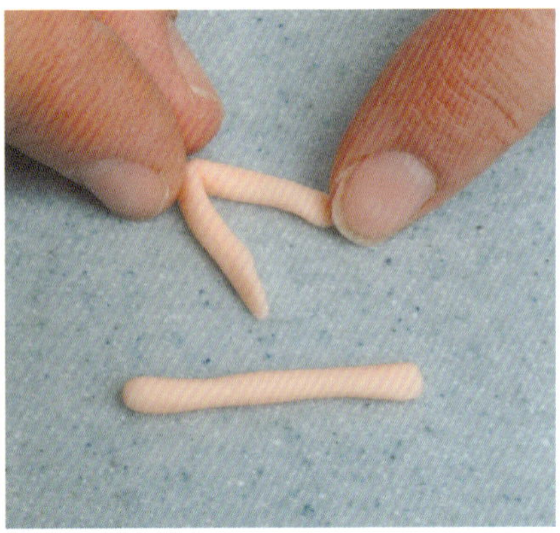

10 Mould small purple triangular shaped bodies. Stick one body onto each pair of legs.

11 Make a tiny flesh coloured ball for each head and stick onto the bodies. Use a drinking straw, held at an angle, to press a smile into the lower part of each face.

12 Make two tiny flesh coloured arms for each fairy and stick into place.

13 To make the eyes place a little black food colour in a dish. Dip the end of a cocktail stick into the colour and carefully dot two tiny spots on each face.

14 Fold a piece of rice paper in half. Cut out a wing shape along the fold. Open it up and you should have identical sized wings. Make a set of wings for each fairy.

15 Colour the remaining buttercream yellow and place a tablespoonful into a piping bag.

16 Fold the bag to close it and carefully snip a tiny triangle off the end. Pipe wiggly hair onto each fairy.

17 Press a set of wings into the back of each fairy to complete your creation.

Vegetable Garden

This has to be one of the simplest cakes to make and everyone loves chocolate finger biscuits. Alternatively you could make chocolate cupcakes and place miniature modelled vegetables on these as a special birthday surprise for someone.

shopping list

- cake sponge 20 x 15cm (8 x 6in)
- cake drum square 30cm (12in)
- sugarpaste chocolate flavoured 1kg (2lb)
- sugarpaste green 250g (9oz)
- sugarpaste white
- marzipan small amount
- chocolate fingers 3 boxes
- desiccated coconut
- chocolate buttercream
- royal icing
- green blossom tint
- cocoa powder
- blossom cutter
- clay gun or tea strainer
- piping tube No. 1

How to make

1 Cover the cake with chocolate buttercream and then chocolate sugarpaste. Spread buttercream onto the side of the cake. Attach the chocolate fingers around the outside of the cake.

2 Cover the board with green sugarpaste. Add white vegetable fat to the rest of the green paste and fit a large mesh disc to the clay gun. Extrude the grass through the mesh or a tea strainer and attach to the board for grass.

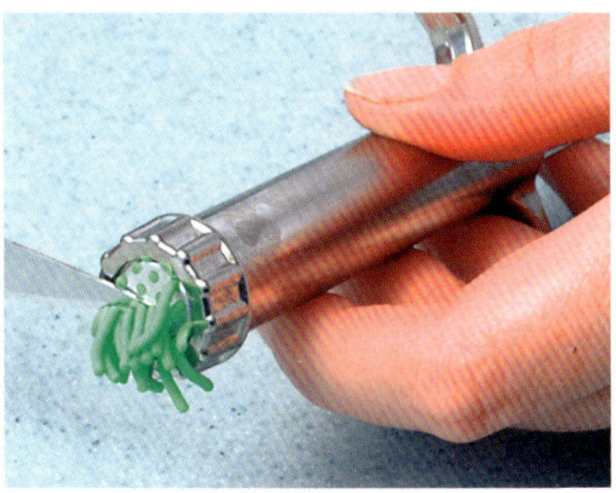

3 Place the coconut into a small bag and add green colour. Shake the bag and add more powder if necessary. Cover the top of the cake with chocolate buttercream, with a fork make the furrows, position the coconut in one corner.

4 Colour 3 different shades of sugarpaste for the blossoms, roll out and cut out. Press the plunger onto the sponge to create the flower. Pipe the centre with a No.1 tube and royal icing and fix in place with royal icing.

5 Colour marzipan orange and shape to form carrots. Extrude dark green marzipan to make the stalks of the carrots.

6 Roll small balls of marzipan in cocoa powder for the potatoes. Tear off pieces of marzipan and join together for the centre of the cauliflower. Flatten small balls of green marzipan to make the leaves for the cabbage and cauliflower.

Howzat

The bat is an ideal place to add an inscription which you can easily make using one of the many alphabet cutters available and modelling paste. This can also be piped in royal icing.

Make matching cupcakes to go with this cake and add tiny sugarpaste bats and balls.

How to make

shopping list

sponge cake 20 x 30cm (8 x 12in)
2 cupcakes
cake board oblong 25 x 56.5cm (10 x 22in)
sugarpaste white 450g (1lb)
sugarpaste light brown 150g (5oz)
sugarpaste chocolate 250g (8oz)
modelling paste 150g (5oz) red
marzipan 150g (5oz)
desiccated coconut 300g (10oz)
3 chocolate coated mini swiss rolls
jam or buttercream

1 Leave the sponge until it is a day old before attempting to cut it. Cut the cake in half lengthways and sandwich together with jam or buttercream.

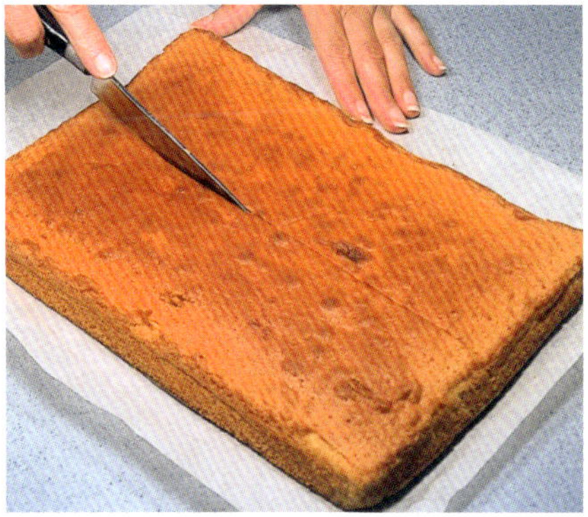

2 To shape the bat cut a slightly slanting slice from the centre of the top cake to halfway down the long sides.

3 Cut off a similar section at both ends, start 5cm (2in) from the ends. Round off the 'toe' of the bat; place on a spare cake board. Spread a thin layer of jam or buttercream over the surface of the cake to help the sugarpaste stick.

4 To achieve the 'wood grain' effect, roll the white and light brown sugarpaste into a sausage shape. Lay them alongside each other lengthwise. Roll them together.

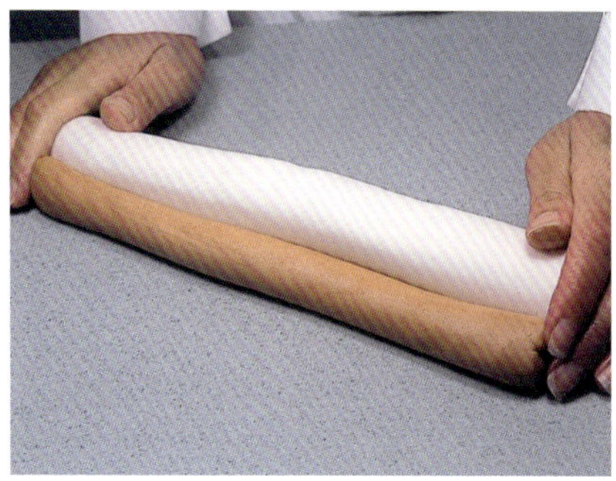

5 Fold in three as shown, roll out into a sausage and fold again. Repeat until you see a marbled effect begin to appear.

6 Lightly dust the work surface with icing sugar and roll out the sugarpaste to about 5mm (1/4in) thick, maintaining a rectangular shape as you roll. You can use spacers to keep the paste at an even thickness when rolling out.

7 Lift the paste with a rolling pin and gently lower over the cake. Smooth and mould the paste to the base. Push in a little to form a cutting line.

8 Cut out a triangle at the top of the bat where it meets the 'handle'. Add dark chocolate paste to the light brown trimmings in the same manner until the wood grain effect is achieved. Roll out the marbled paste (use spacers to gain the correct depth) and cut to size.

9 Trim the ends off the mini swiss rolls so that they fit neatly together, brush with apricot glaze to help the sugarpaste stick. Roll out chocolate sugarpaste into a rectangle and use to coat the swiss rolls.

10 Lift the handle and turn it, so that when you put it down on the cake board the sealed edge is underneath. Smooth and mould the end of the handle to the 'shoulder' of the bat, as shown.

11 Slice the top off each cupcake and join together with apricot glaze to make a ball, then brush more glaze over it. Cover with marzipan and smooth around the shape, pulling up a pleat. Cut this pleat away and smooth the join closed. Sit inside a nylon sieve placed over a jug (see page 46).

12 Brush the marzipan with clear alcohol and apply red modelling paste as in step 11. It is worth spending time over this as it will affect your overall finish. Whilst the paste is still soft emboss a line of stitching with a stitch wheel.

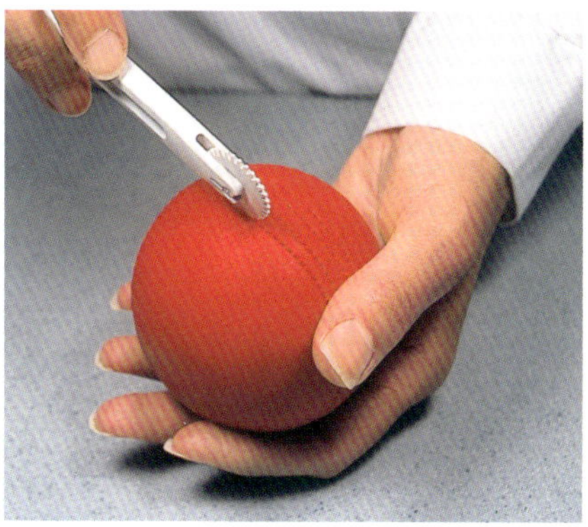

13 Place the desiccated coconut into a polythene bag with some green food colouring. Hold the bag closed and rub the colour into the coconut.

14 Paint the board with sugar glue and spoon the 'grass' evenly on the board, pushing it close up to the cricket bat and ball. Finally edge the cake board with ribbon, making it slightly higher than the board edge to stop the coconut falling out.

Ballet Positions

For a boy's cake look for suitable images of knights or pirates and transfer these to the cake. Add white sparkles over grey colour for a sparkly metallic finish for the armour and the pirate's sword.

How to make

Preparation

Trace the ballerina pattern (see page 47). The same head and tutu will be used for each ballerina.

shopping list

sponge cake 25 x 20cm (10 x 8in)
cake board 35 x 25cm (14 x 10in)
sugarpaste 1.3kg (3lb)
mexican paste 150g (5oz)
royal icing 50g (2oz)
magic sparkles
set of bow cutters

1 Ice the board and crimp the board edge. Ice the cake and place on the board. Colour 100g of mexican paste pink, 25g lilac and 25g flesh. Roll long sausages of paste and attach around the cake base with sugar glue. Crimp and leave to dry.

2 Grease the large bow cutter and the non-stick rolling board with white fat. Roll out pink mexican paste thinly. Do not lift and turn once rolled. Press the cutter firmly onto paste. Remove the cutter and surplus paste. Cut out another three bows and place on a sponge pad to dry.

3 Roll out pink mexican paste and cut out the front loops of the bow only. Trim with a knife if needed. Roll lightly across the loops to stretch them slightly. Brush sugar glue along the left and right edges on the cut-out bow's front loops and then place the extra loops in position. Leave to dry.

4 Cut out small pieces of mexican paste 2 x 1.25cm and place over a small rolling pin to dry.

5 Cut out the tutu and head from the tracing paper. Grease the non-stick rolling board with white fat. Roll out pink mexican paste and cut out three tutus. Repeat with lilac but only cut out two.

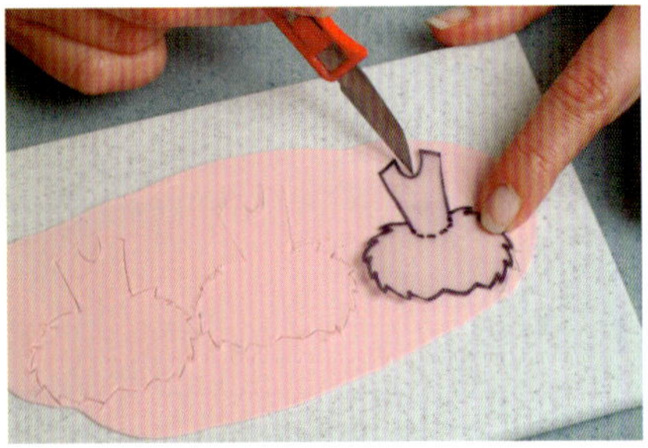

6 Position the tutus on the cake starting with a pink one in the centre. Do not attach with sugar glue until all are evenly spaced.

7 Roll out flesh mexican paste, cut out five heads and attach to the cake.

8 Cut out one set of arms and legs at a time from the tracing paper, then cut out in flesh mexican paste and attach to the cake. When the leg is cut out in flesh include the shoe and then cut out the coloured shoe to attach on top.

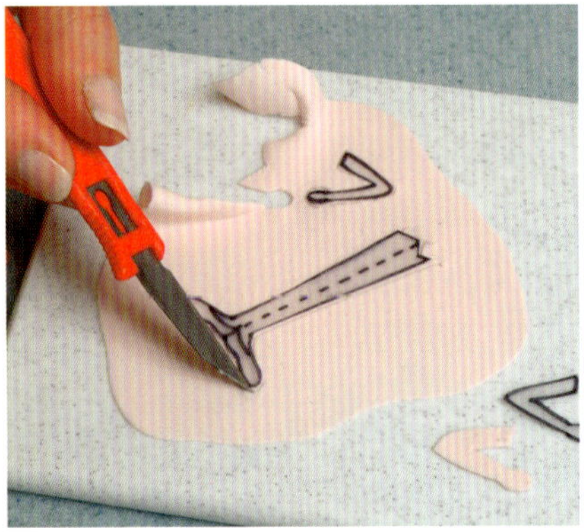

9 Cut out very small squares of coloured mexican paste for hair bobbles and attach. Dust the bodice and ballet shoes lightly with white satin.

10 Place 1 tablespoon of white royal icing in a piping bag with a No.1 nozzle. Pipe an edge to the crimping around the cake and board.

11 Colour the remaining royal icing pale grey. Place 1 tablespoon in a piping bag with a No.1 nozzle and the rest in a bag with a No.2. Use the No.2 to pipe the outlines. Add details, i.e. eyes, mouth, hair. Use the No.1 for the shoe ribbons. Pipe positions and the child's name with the No.2. Leave to dry.

12 Mix silver powder with isopropyl alcohol and paint the grey piping and the crimped edges. Keep the brush at a low angle to the cake (not like you would hold a pen) to help avoid mistakes or smudges.

13 Paint sugar glue very thinly over tutu skirts. When just tacky sprinkle over the appropriate coloured magic sparkles. Ease into place with a dry paintbrush.

14 Grind the remaining pink Magic Sparkles in the pot to a fine powder glitter with the end of a teaspoon handle.

15 Brush the bows and the ribbons thinly with sugar glue. Fold a piece of greaseproof paper in half then open out. Sprinkle the glitter over the bows and ribbons above the paper, turn bows over and tap lightly. Leave to dry. The sparkles should now pour off the paper and back into the pot.

NOTE: Magic Sparkles should only be applied to damp rather than wet areas. They will dissolve if too much sugar glue or water is used.

16 Attach the bows and ribbon loops to the cake with a little white royal icing.

17 Dampen a pastry brush with water and brush lightly over the iced board. When almost dry, sprinkle with white Magic Sparkles.

Butterfly Extravaganza

As well as a wedding this cake could be made for a birthday party. Change the colours of the flowers and ribbon to create a totally different look from pale delicate pastels to bold vibrant colours.

How to make

Preparation

Cover the cake boards with sugarpaste and the fruit cake with marzipan and leave to dry for a couple of days. Cover the fruit cake with sugarpaste and place on the smaller board, secure with a little royal icing. Use a glue stick to attach the thick ribbon around the edge of both boards.

shopping list

- square fruit cake 15cm (6in)
- 12 small square sponge cakes 5 x 5cm (2 x 2in)
- marzipan 1.3kg (2lb 14oz)
- buttercream
- square cake drums 20, 28cm (8, 11in)
- thin cake card cut into squares 12 x 5cm (2in)
- purple ribbon 4 metres x 7mm, 2 metres x 16mm
- ivory sugarpaste 2kg (4lb 8oz)
- cream flower paste
- butterfly cutters
- assorted small flower cutters

1 Thinly roll out cream flower paste. Press the butterfly cutters firmly into the paste. Lift and carefully remove the excess paste. Cover the butterflies so they do not dry out. You will need 2 large and 12 medium butterflies.

2 Dust the back and front of the butterflies with a burgundy and lilac shimmer dust. Brush empress purple on the tips of the butterfly and dust mother of pearl over the top. Paint in the head and bodies with black food colour mixed with alcohol.

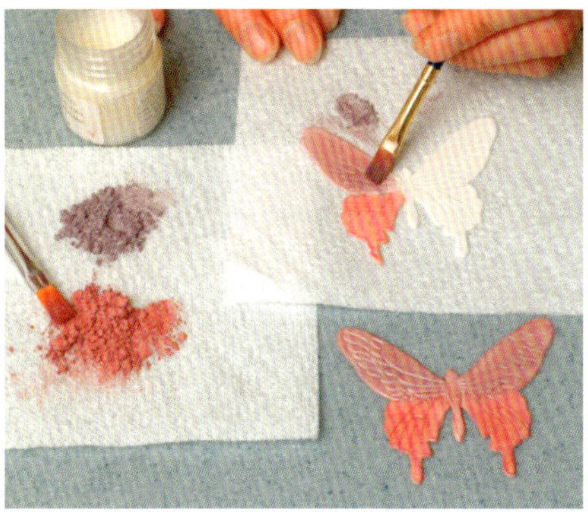

3 Carefully place the butterflies in a piece of folded card to shape and support them and leave to dry.

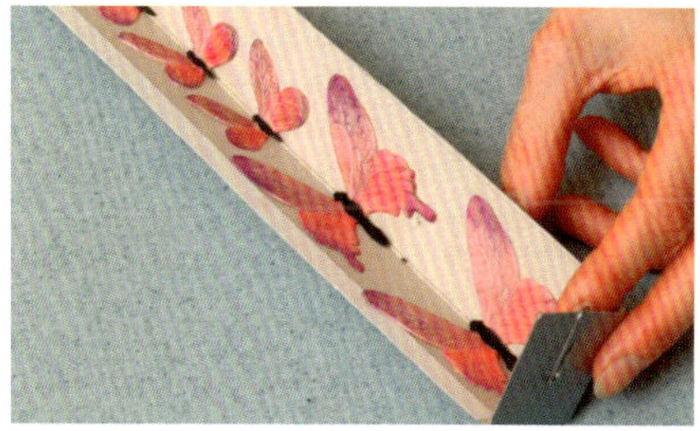

4 Thinly roll out cream flower paste and cut out a selection of flowers. Dust the flower heads with a variety of dusting colours.

5 Place the flowers onto a sponge pad. Gently use a ball tool to cup and shape the larger sized flowers.

6 Use paste food colour mixed with alcohol to paint with a fine brush long, quick upward brush strokes around the bottom of the cake to represent grass. Vary the width of the strokes and the intensity of the colour.

7 Attach a ribbon around the base of the cake with piping gel. Paint in a flower stem. With a fine paintbrush paint a series of violet dots to create the flower head.

8 With a No.1 tube pipe a pale green flower stem close to the painted flower, start about the same height as the flower head. Pipe down to just above the top of the ribbon.

9 Attach a flower head with royal icing and pipe in the centre (No. 1 tube). Continue around the sides and vary the flower heights.

10 Thinly roll out pale green flower paste and cut into long thin triangles. Place on a pad and gently use a ball tool to shape and curl. Attach with sugar glue to the cake. Add the flower heads and small butterflies.

11 Apply a little edible glue to one side and attach pieces either side of the piped stems just above the ribbon. Continue around the sides of the cake. Glue on two small butterflies above the flowers to finish each side.

12 Cover the sponge cakes with a thin layer of buttercream and marzipan. Leave to dry overnight and then cover with sugarpaste. Attach ribbon around the base of each with royal icing.

13 Pipe a little icing underneath the body of each small butterfly and attach to the top of the individual cakes, alternate the angle and the colours.

14 Attach the two large butterflies at different angles to the top of the cake. Support with small pieces of sponge as they dry.

15 Place the cake separator in the centre of the board and the cakes around it. Line them up evenly with the edge of the board. Secure each one with a little royal icing.

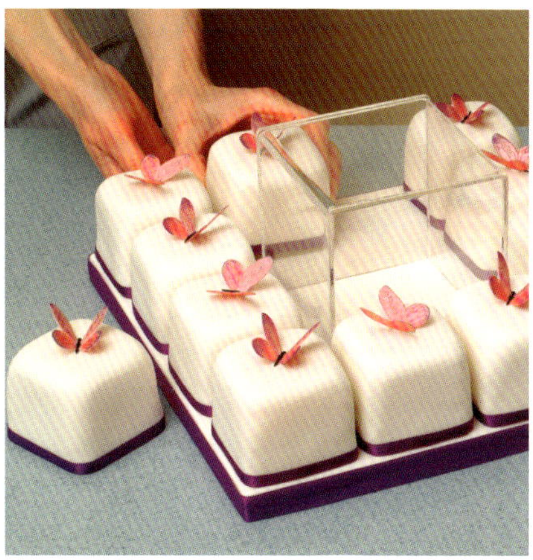

16 Position the top tier to finish.

Celebrate

This cake can be used for so many special occasions from a birthday to a New Year party. Replace the top candle with 'push in' letters and numbers made especially for cakes. These can be used to spell out a name or 'Happy Birthday'.

You could emboss patterns on the parcels for a simple finish, rather than piping if you are short of time (cut the parcel shape after you have embossed the paste) .

How to make

shopping list

round sponge cakes 15, 20cm (6, 8in)
sugarpaste 1.5kg (3lb)
buttercream 500g (1lb)
round cake card 15cm (6in)
round cake drum 30cm (12in)
royal icing

1 Place the 8in round sponge cake on a 12in round cake drum towards the back of the board. Place the 6in sponge onto a thin cake card.

2 Mask the cakes with buttercream.

3 Cover the 8in sponge cake with white sugarpaste, including the board.

4 Use your hands to shape the sugarpaste to the cake.

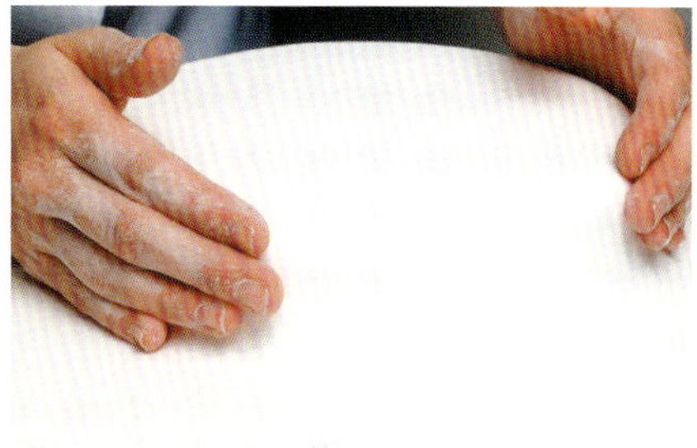

5 Use a smoother like an iron to get a neat finish and trim away the excess sugarpaste.

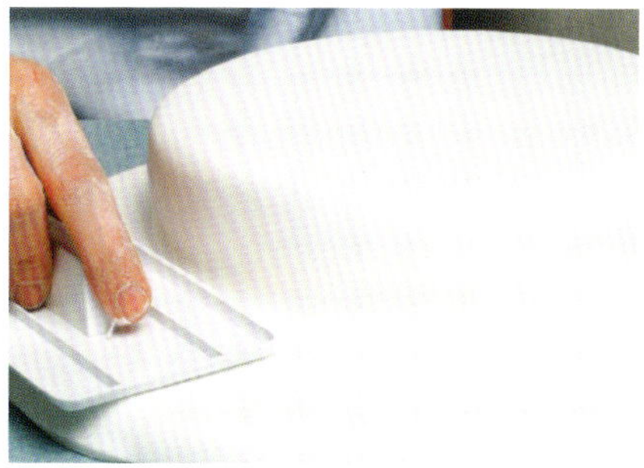

6 Crimp around the edge of the board.

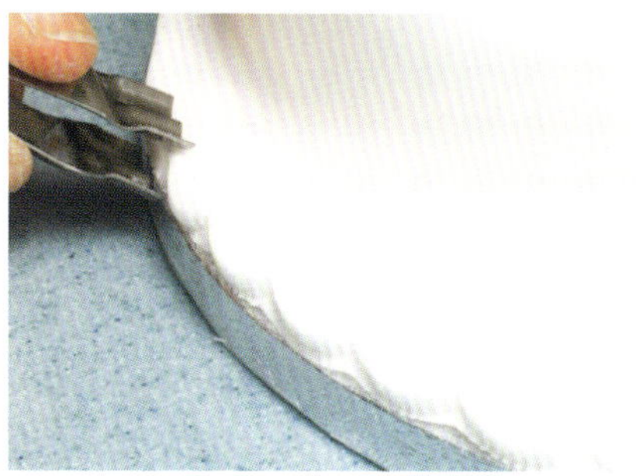

7 To prevent the top of the cake sinking into the bottom you will need to dowel the bottom tier. 4 dowels need to be located just inside the edge of the cake board from the above tier.

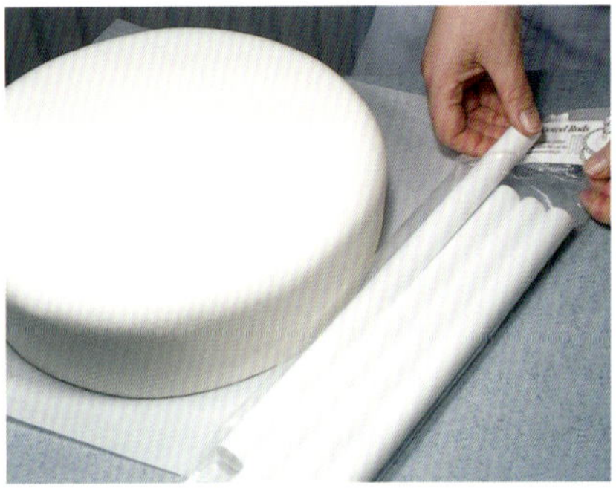

8 Gently push the dowel into the cake until it reaches the board. Mark the dowels $^1/_8$in above the cake surface. Pull the dowels out and cut to the size of the longest one (to ensure a level cake surface) with a knife. Replace the dowels.

9 Cover the 6in sponge cake with white sugarpaste, place towards the back of the 8in cake. Place a small amount of royal icing in the centre of the cake.

10 Roll out a variety of different coloured sugarpaste. Cut out various sizes of squares and rectangles to create the parcels and candles. Allow to set.

11 Stick the parcels and candles onto the side of the cake with royal icing. Pipe different patterns onto the parcels with royal icing in a bag fitted with a No.1 tube.

12 Pipe in a royal icing black wick on the candles.

13 Marble red and yellow sugarpaste and cut out with a calyx cutter. Trim with a craft knife to make the flames.

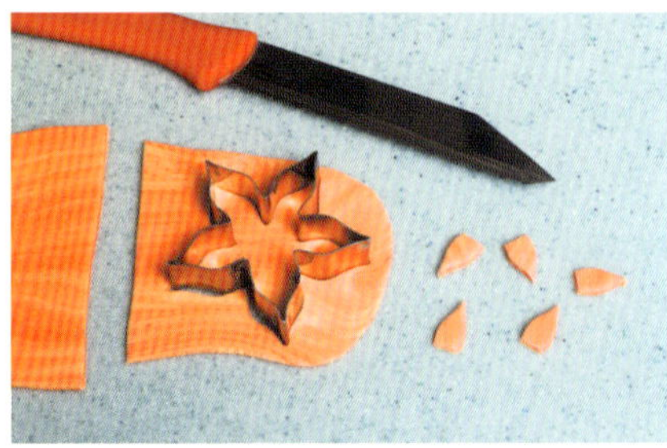

14 Paint the centre of the flame using red food colouring. Paint various patterns onto the candles with food colouring.

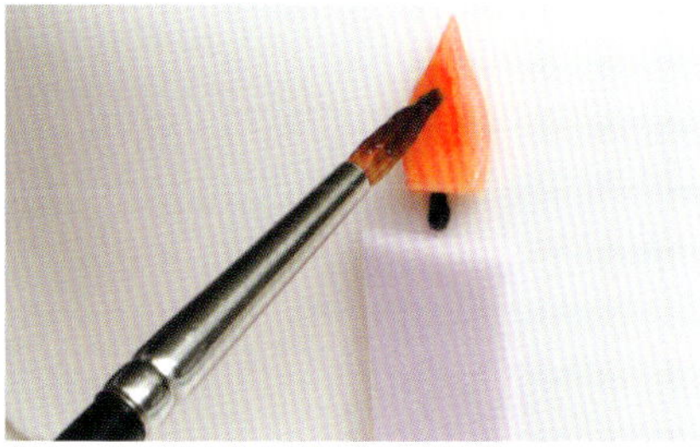

15 Roll out various colours of sugarpaste and cut thin strips. Wrap strips around the end of a paintbrush to create coloured streamers.

16 Place the streamers around the edge of the 6in sponge cake and secure with royal icing.

17 Roll two fairly thick sausage shapes out of lilac and yellow sugarpaste. Twist them together and roll into a smooth thick cylinder, trim both ends and stand it upright.Paint a short piece of spaghetti black and insert in the candle top. Marble yellow and red sugarpaste together, mould a

small pear shape, press flat and twist. Place on the spaghetti; paint the centre of the flame red. Place the candle in the centre of the cake and secure with royal icing.

18 Roll various colours of sugarpaste into balls and place

them onto hooked 30g wires. Push a smaller ball onto the wire to create the base of the balloon. Leave until set.

19 Roll out various colours of sugarpaste and cut narrow strips, twist them slightly and thread them onto a 30g wire. Leave to dry.

20 Place a flower pick behind the candle and insert the balloons and twists.

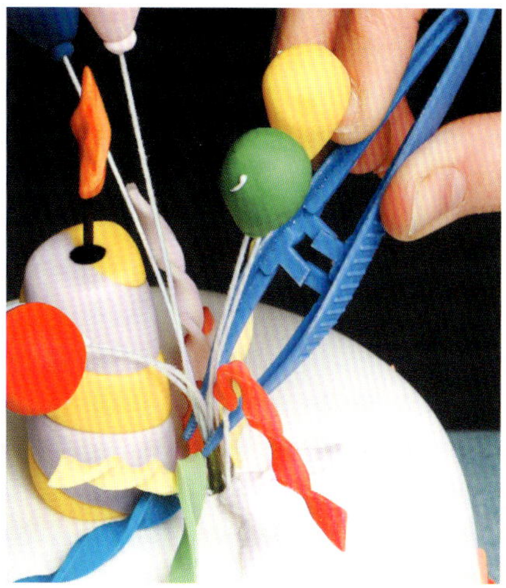

Daisy Wedding Cake

The appeal of this elegant wedding cake is in its simple daisy design which gives it a fresh springtime feel.

The daisy motif could be transferred onto cupcakes or even cookies and given as favours to the wedding guests.

shopping list

fruit or sponge cakes round 15, 23cm (6, 9in) covered and stacked
cake drum 30cm (12in)
daisy/6 petal cutters
piping tubes No. 1, 1.5
bead maker
gold wire 26 gauge

How to make

1 Cut out several daisies with the largest two cutters of the set and leave to dry on a piece of foam. Roll out the paste again, but thinner this time, and attach randomly to the sides of both cakes.

2 To finish pipe a coil in the centre of the flowers at the beginning of the petals with royal icing and a No.1.5 tube.

3 Pipe outlines onto the flowers and when dry attach a piece of gold wire to the back. Pipe outlines on to the cake daisies.

4 Tilt the cake and pipe simple line scrolls with yellow icing and a No.1 tube. Begin with the coil and then lift the tube away from the cake to give the long scroll. Pipe random dots between the scrolls.

5 Dust the inside of the bead maker with silver snow lustre dust. Roll flower paste into a long sausage and place in the bead maker. Press down firmly and remove the excess paste. Let the beads fall out of the mould and attach to the cake with edible glue.

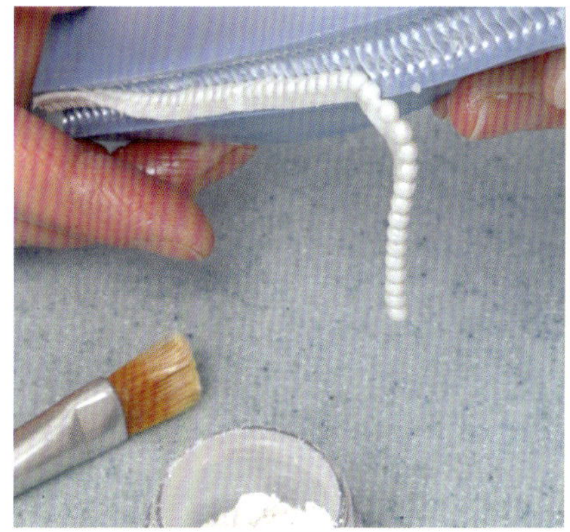

6 Insert a small piece of oasis fix into the top of the small flower pick. Insert the flower pick into the centre of the top tier. Insert the wired daisies into the oasis fix.

Top Hat

Instead of piping the initial stamp one out of flower paste. An inscription could also be piped on the cake top.

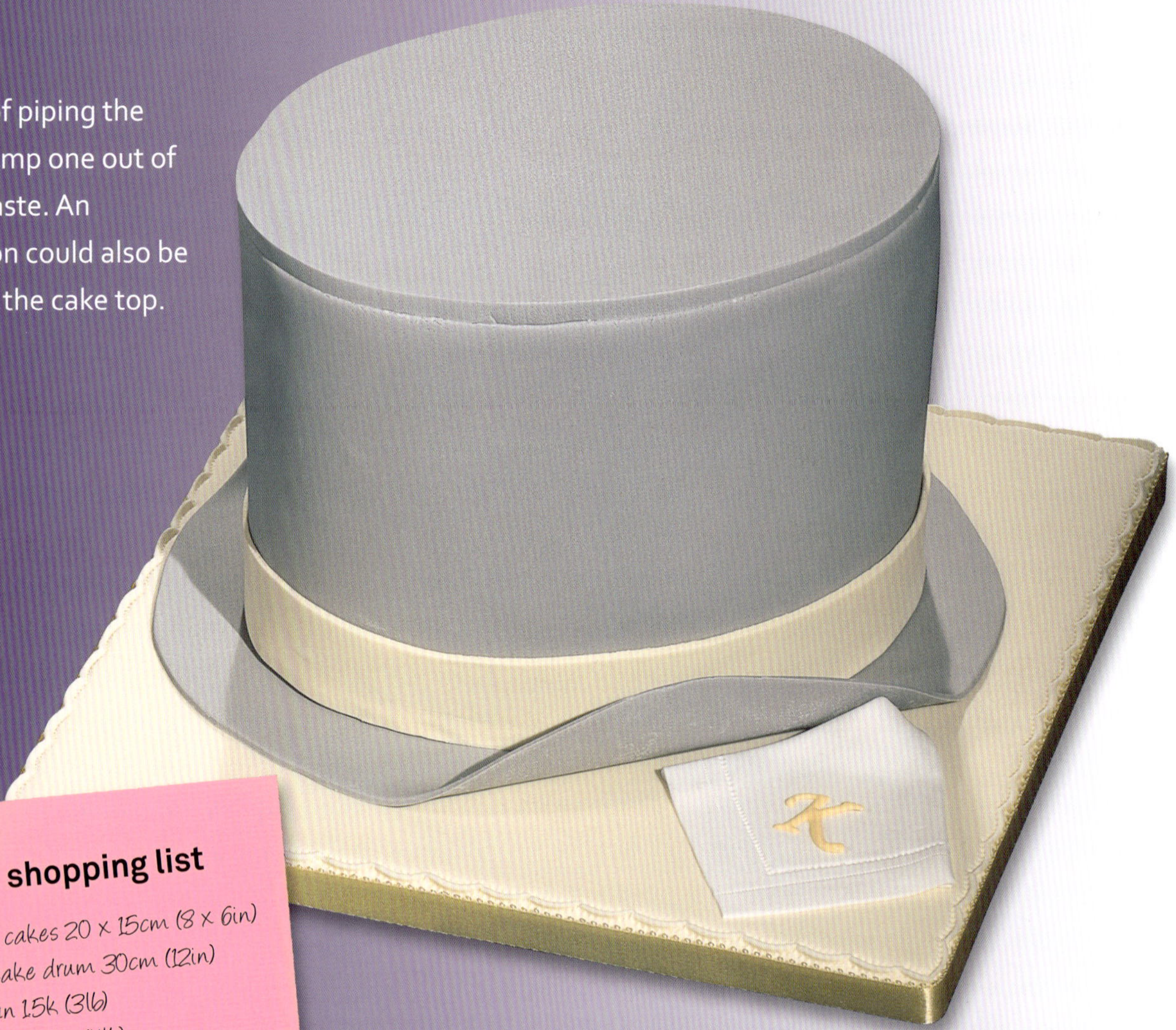

shopping list

- two oval cakes 20 x 15cm (8 x 6in)
- square cake drum 30cm (12in)
- marzipan 1.5k (3lb)
- sugarpaste 2kg (4lb)
- royal icing
- flower paste
- piping tube No. 1

How to make

1 Place the cakes on top of each other and level them. Cover the sides and then the top with marzipan (see page 7). Roll out grey sugarpaste to the length and width of the sides of the cake. Roll up the paste and attach around the cake, place the join at the back.

2 Make a paper template of the cake top. Roll out a piece of sugarpaste and attach to the cake top. Out of yellow 50:50 paste cut out a ribbon

and attach to the cake, keep all the joins at the back of the cake.

3 Measure the cake and make a template for the hat brim which is 2in larger than the cake. Cut out the shape from 50:50 paste. Curve the sides upwards and use formers to hold the sides in place. Leave to dry.

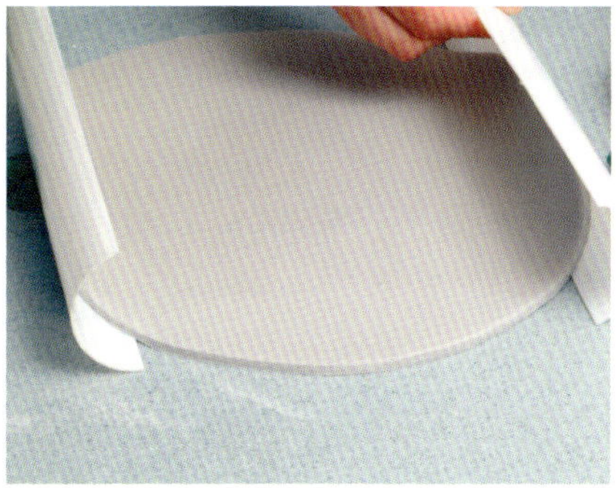

4 Roll out a 4in square of white 50:50 paste. Emboss a line of stitches 1cm from the edge. Make a line of holes with the piping tube 1cm further in. Turn over and fold in the sides and allow to dry.

5 Draw an initial and place under a silicone sheet. Fill a piping bag with yellow royal icing. Cut a tiny hole and pressure pipe the letter (squeeze the icing out so it fills the shape). Use a paintbrush to form any points and leave to dry under an Anglepoise lamp.

6 Place the rim onto the board and secure the cake in the centre. Attach the handkerchief and the letter with royal icing.

Beach Bag and Matching Flip-Flops

If you are feeling adventurous make a pair of sunglasses and a beach towel and add these to the top oval of paste so they look as if they are coming out of the bag. You can also change the colours and type of flowers.

shopping list

- oval cakes 2, 15 x 20cm (6 x 8in)
- square cake drum 30cm (12in)
- buttercream 500g (1lb)
- sugarpaste 2.5kg (5lb)
- mexican paste 500g (1lb)
- gum tragacanth (GT)
- six petal daisy cutter
- oval cutter/template 12.5cm x 8xm (5 x 3in)

How to make

1 Place the oval cutter on the cakes. Using this as a guide shape the cakes with a sharp knife. Apply buttercream to the centre and sides, then coat with a thin layer of sugarpaste.

2 Mix 1 teaspoon of GT into 1kg of green sugarpaste. Roll the paste out thinly and cut a rectangle. Fold under the long sides, make pleats with a skewer under the paste and attach to the cake. Roll a strip of paste and add to the bag top, use an oval piece for the very top.

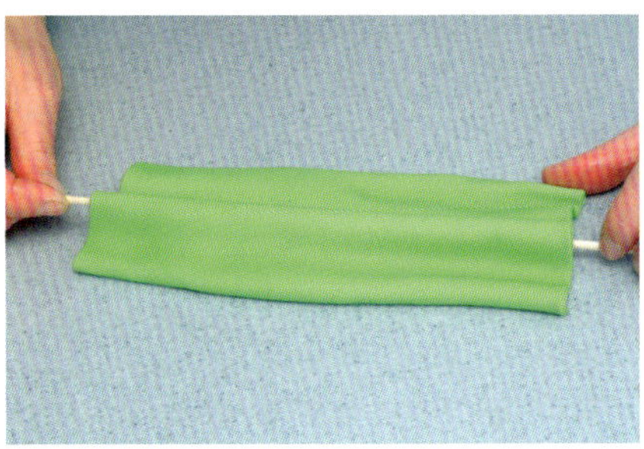

3 Cut out white daisies from mexican paste, add pink centres and attach to the bag. Soften sugarpaste with white vegetable fat and place in a clay gun fitted with a shamrock die. Extrude paste and twist to make the handle, attach to the bag with sugar glue.

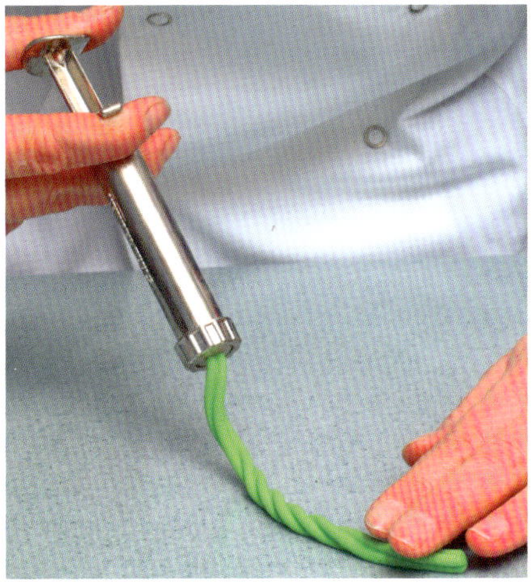

4 Roll out pink sugarpaste $^{1}/_{2}$cm thick and cut around the flip-flop template (see page 47). Cut a tiny hole for the toe separator and insert a small green sausage of paste.

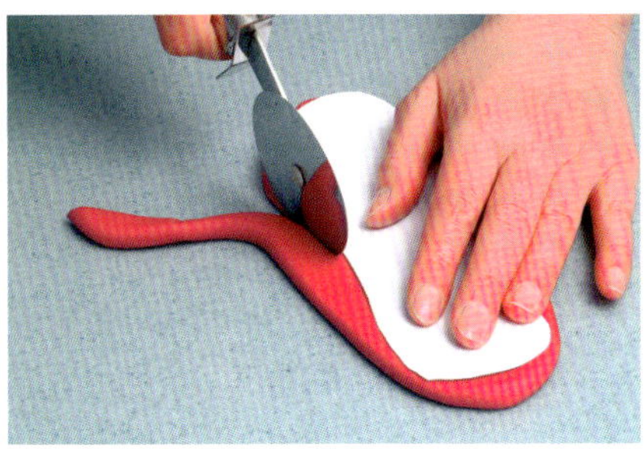

5 Make daisies with pink centres and attach to the flip-flops.

6 Emboss lines into strips of green paste, cut and attach to the flip-flops. Allow to dry as shown.

DIY

A totally different birthday cake for a DIY enthusiast. If you are short of time buy two large swiss rolls to make this cake.

Vary the design by using different colours or match their wallpaper for a very striking cake! This is a fun cake to make where you can apply your own design ideas and you can also add a suitable inscription onto the cake board.

shopping list

- jumbo swiss rolls x 2
- sugarpaste 3kg (6lb)
- cake drum square 35cm (14in)
- stencil of choice
- piping tube No.2
- circle cutters

How to make

1 Cut a circle of paste the size of the end of the swiss roll and mark the centre with the piping tube. Emboss concentric rings around the centre with different sizes of circle.

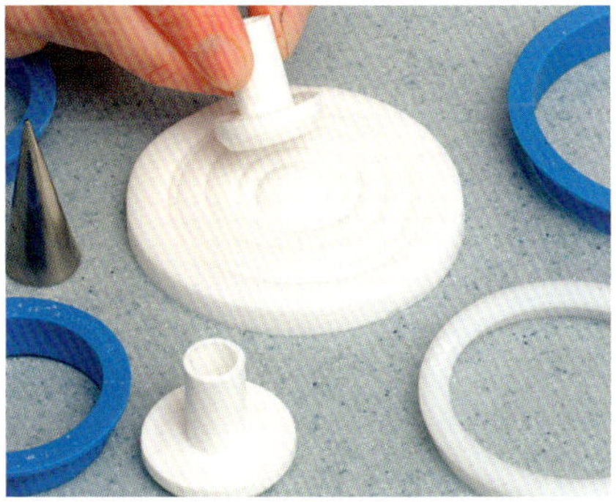

2 Cover the rest of the cake with buttercream and place onto a piece of rolled out sugarpaste. Roll the cake up in the icing, smooth the surface and place the join underneath the cake. Leave to dry for a couple of days.

3 Attach the stencil to the cake with micropore tape. Mix a small amount of powder with a small amount of vegetable fat and use a flat brush to fill in the colour.

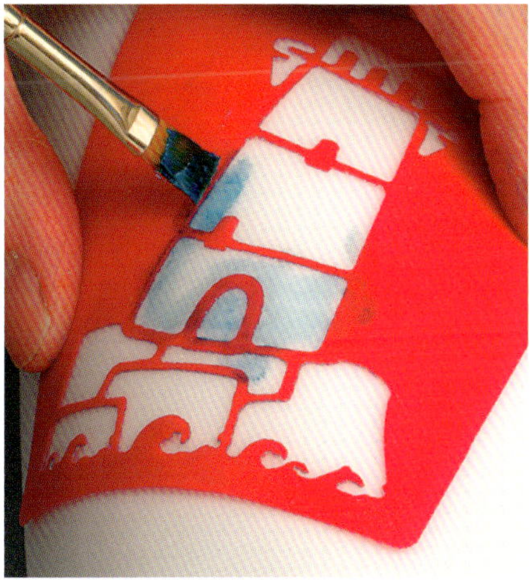

4 Mix a small amount of ice blue paste colour with alcohol. Apply the colour onto the cake with a sponge. Add a touch of navy and shade the wallpaper with this.

5 To make the brush mix an equal quantity of flower paste into the white icing. Colour with ivory paste colour and mould into a handle shape. Use a piping tube to create the hole. When dry, paint the wood grain effect and glaze.

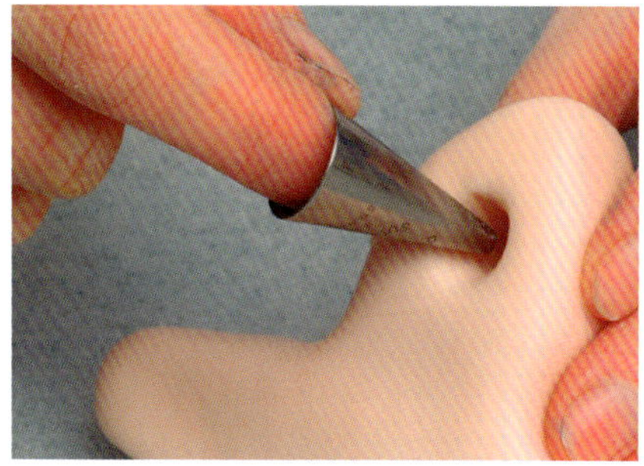

6 Make the bristles from black 50:50 paste. Form the paste into a rectangle the length of the handle. Mark in the bristles with a knife and texture the end with the No. 2 piping tube. Fix everything to the pre-coated board with royal icing or softened sugarpaste.

Snowman Family

This little snowman family look cosy in their winter woolies! The bas relief snowmen are shaped very simply before their co-ordinated hats and scarves (or shawl) are added.

This cake could also be made from sponge or you could make cupcakes, cover them with a blue disc of sugarpaste and a scaled-down snowman.

How to make

Preparation

Marzipan the cake and ice with the blue sugarpaste. Ice the board with white sugarpaste.

shopping list

round rich fruit cake 25cm (10in)
marzipan 1.3kg (3lb)
sugarpaste 18kg (4lb)
blue sugarpaste 1.3kg (3lb)
royal icing or softened sugarpaste
magic sparkles-white
size guide
piping tube No. 43

1 The size guide is used to help achieve the correct size for each modelled part. Roll a ball of paste and place in the required hole in the size guide. The ball of paste is the correct size when it sits two thirds above the hole and one third below.

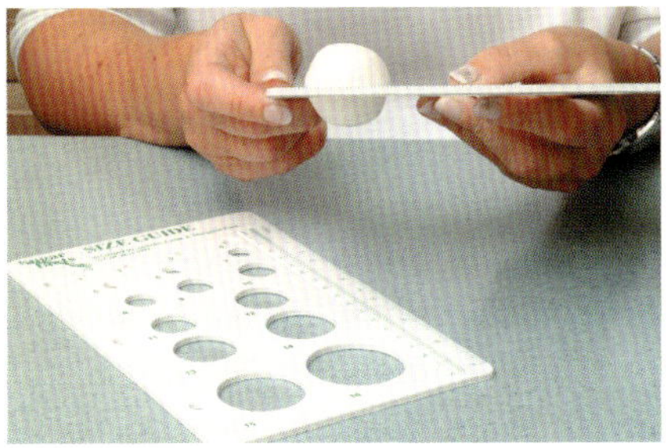

2 Use the size guide to mould four pear-shaped bodies from the following size pieces of sugarpaste. Dad 16, Mum 15, Boy 14 and Girl 13. Flatten each shape slightly and attach to the cake with water. Indent buttonholes with a ball tool. Roll small balls of coloured paste for the buttons and attach.

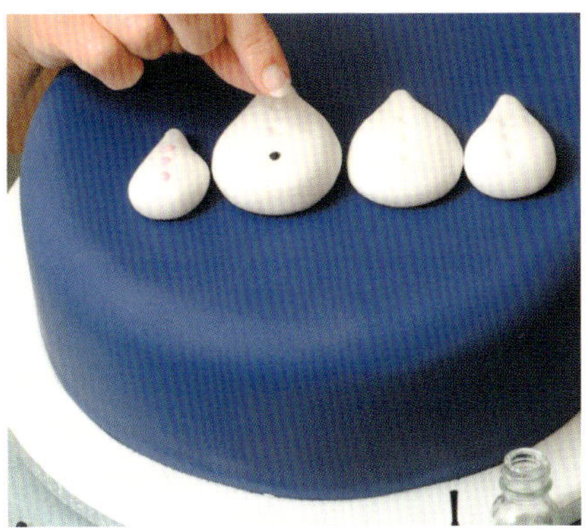

3 Shape each arm from these sizes: Dad 10, Mum 9 and Girl 8 (half for each arm). Leave the boy until later. For each arm roll a sausage shape and pinch slightly thinner at one end, mark with a dresden tool where the elbow bends and attach to the bodies.

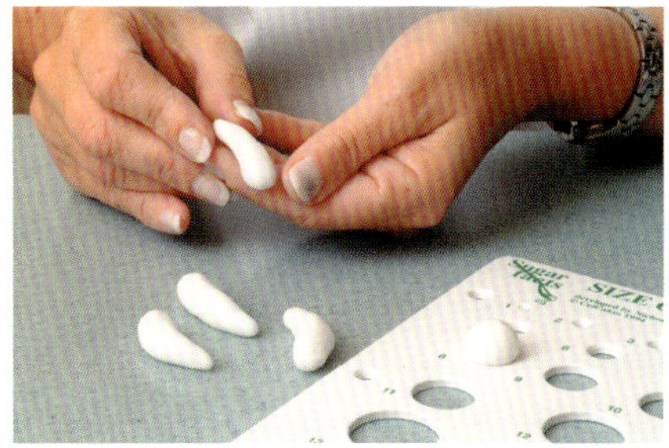

4 The head sizes are: Dad 14, Mum 13, Boy 12 and Girl 11. Flatten each ball of paste slightly and attach. Use a ball tool to indent the nose and eyes. Use a mouth tool to emboss the mouth. Add tiny balls of black paste for the eyes and small carrots of orange paste for noses. Add a tiny circle of pale pink sugarpaste to the girl's and mum's cheeks. Use powder colours mixed with water to paint highlights and eyelashes on the eyes.

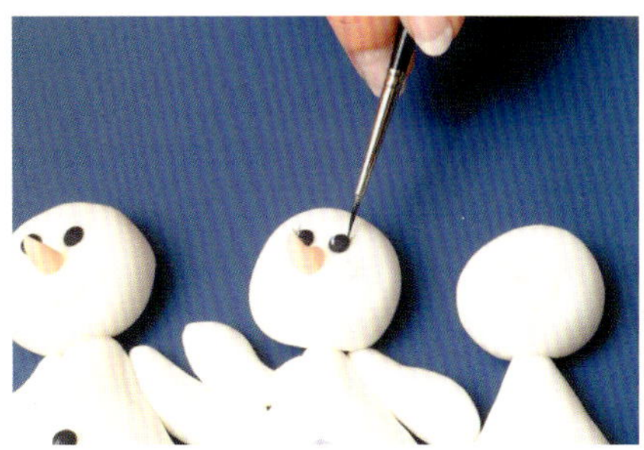

5 For the scarves cut a straight piece of sugarpaste with a cutting wheel. Cut these into three pieces (two long, one short). Mark fringes with a dresden tool and pattern with a stitch wheel. Pinch the top end of the long pieces together and both ends of the short piece and attach.

6 Trace and cut out the shawl pattern (see page 47). Check the size before cutting out and alter if necessary. Place over rolled-out sugarpaste and cut out. Mark a knitted pattern with a dresden tool. Check the fit again before attaching.

7 To make earmuffs, attach a band of pink sugarpaste over the girl's head and a ball of sugarpaste either side.

8 Push small pieces of pink sugarpaste through a sieve and trim with a knife. Keep on the knife blade as close as possible to the girl. Use a cocktail stick to slide the paste off and on to the earmuff. Secure by pressing into place with the cocktail stick. Repeat until the earmuff is covered.

9 Mum and Dad's hats are each shaped from size 12 pieces of sugarpaste. Shape and attach to their heads. Attach a thin sausage of paste around the mum's shawl and the edge of her hat. For the trim repeat instructions for the girl's earmuffs.

10 Attach a white sugarpaste ball and a sausage to the dad's hat for trim and bobble. To make fur soften 150g of sugarpaste with water and brush a little of this over the trim and bobble.

11 Flatten a semi-circle of paste for the boy's hat. Roll a small ball of paste and shape a peak for the front.

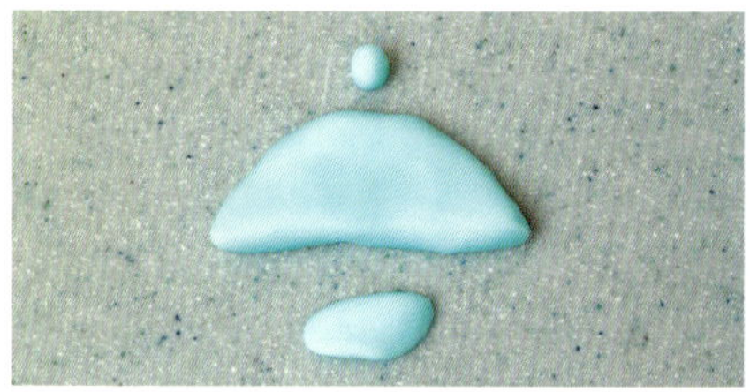

12 Attach the hat to the boy's head. Use a dresden tool to mark a knitted pattern on the hat. Finish by attaching the bobble and the peak. Brush sugar glue over each body. Cover the bodies with finely ground Magic Sparkles.

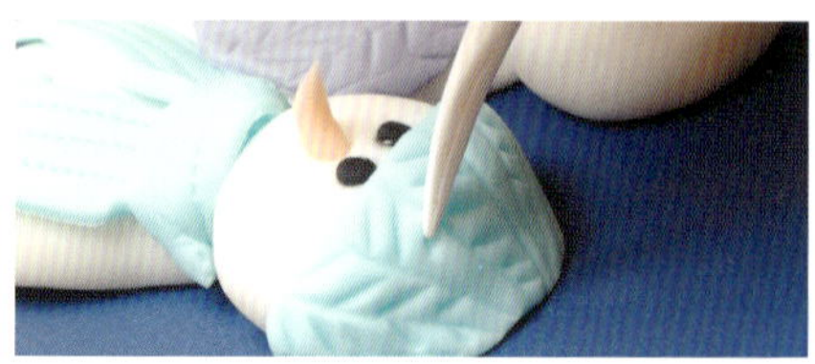

13 Brush snowflake lustre dust over hats, scarves, shawl and earmuffs. Be very careful on the shawl trim etc.

14 Place a 15ml spoonful of softened sugarpaste in a piping bag and trim the end. Pipe roughly below the snowmen then spread with a damp paintbrush. Place cake over greaseproof paper and sprinkle with large flakes of the Magic Sparkles over the rough snow beneath the snowmen. Remove excess with a paintbrush and pour off the paper back into the pot.

15 Use royal icing or sugarpaste softened with water to pipe various sizes of dots randomly over the top and around the sides of the cake for snow. Pipe approximately 10 dots at a time.

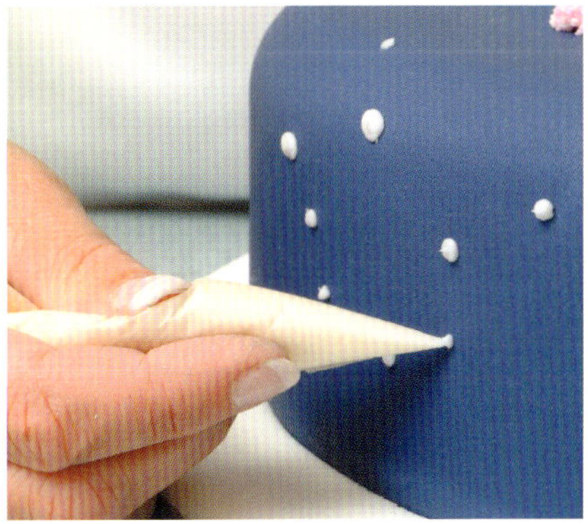

16 Place the cake back onto the greaseproof paper. Scoop some fine sparkles onto your finger and gently touch the piped snow. If the snow is drying too quickly for the sparkles to stick brush on a little sugar glue.

17 Use a large brush to spread sugar glue thinly over the iced board. Sprinkle the larger flake sparkles over the board and spread gently with your finger if needed.

18 Place softened sugarpaste in a piping bag with a No. 43 nozzle and pipe shells around the base of the cake. They can then be sprinkled with the fine sparkles to finish.

Noël

Create this classic chequerboard style cake for Christmas. You can vary this design by changing the colours of the gold squares to lilac and placing silver Christmas motifs in the spaces along with silver lettering on the squares. The squares could also be textured for a different look.

shopping list

- square fruit cake 20cm (8in)
- cake board square 30cm (12in)
- sugarpaste red 500g (1lb)
- modelling paste 250g (8oz)
- square cutter 4.5cm
- robin, bell, holly cutters

How to make

1 Place the coated cake on the board. Cover the board with strips of red paste, mitre at the corners and smooth over to hide the joins. Leave to dry overnight. Attach green ribbon to the cake sides.

2 Roll a long sausage of sugarpaste and secure to the cake with water. Overlap the sausage and cut through both pieces for a perfect join.

3 Roll out the modelling paste 3mm ($^{1}/_{8}$in) thick and place on a flat board. Cut out 4.5cm squares with a cutter or a cardboard template. Remove the excess paste carefully so the shape is not distorted. Allow to dry overnight. Apply a very thin even layer of Gildesol, apply brilliant gold metallic lustre dust and burnish with a soft brush. Attach the gold squares to the cake with edible glue.

4 Roll out red modelling paste and cut out the letters N, O, E and L, leave these to dry on a sponge pad. Roll out green modelling paste and cut out 14 holly leaves. Twist the leaves and leave to dry on dimpled foam or crunched up foil. Brush confectioners varnish on these when they are dry. Make 18 red berries.

5 Colour modelling paste brown and cut out a robin. Cut out another one in red paste. Use a small circle cutter to remove the red breast and secure this with water to the robin. Dip the end of a cocktail stick in black paste colour and use this to dot the eye.

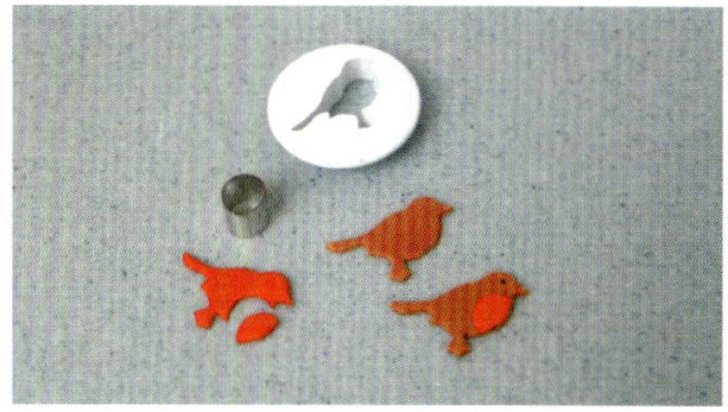

6 Cut two trees and two bells. Use a tiny round cutter to stamp out a circle. Cut the circle in half and use this for the bell clapper, colour gold like the squares.

7 Use edible glue and a fine paintbrush to dab a very small amount of the glue onto the back of each letter and position as shown. Complete the cake by securing all the decorations in place with edible glue.

Hints and tips

To coat a cake with buttercream cover the sides first. This allows you to hold the top of the cake to keep it steady without getting your fingers too sticky.

Take this book to your local sugarcraft shop so they can advise you what to buy for your chosen project(s).

To get a really smooth coating on sugarpaste iron the surface with a pair of smoothers. For awkward cake shapes place your fingers in a piece of sugarpaste and use this to smooth the sugarpaste covered cake.

Use a soft, very slightly damp paintbrush to lightly brush away any dusty icing sugar marks. The sugarpaste will look shiny initially but it will dry and revert to a matt finish.

To make flesh coloured paste add a touch of chestnut and rose paste colour to white sugarpaste. Add to this a touch of melon or brown/black for other skin tones.

You will find crimpers are easier to use if you slip a rubber band around them so they are 5mm ($^1/_4$in) apart. Dip into icing sugar and then into the paste, pinch and release. Re-dip every few pinches.

Drinking straws can be used to make a smiley or sad mouth.

To make mini square cakes you can buy specially designed cake tins or cut up a square sponge cake. Bake the sponge cakes in advance and freeze them. They are also easier to work with when they are frozen.

When marbling paste take care not to overwork it, three or four rolls is probably sufficient. Stop before it turns completely the same colour all over. Check the underneath as sometimes the marble patterns are even better there. If you do happen to over-work the colours simply re-knead more coloured paste back into it.

When two cupcakes are joined together with apricot glaze for the cricket ball they will not form a perfect shape. Adjust this as you add the marzipan coating.

Another way to make the cricket ball is to crumble spare cake trimmings, add chopped nuts and cherries, moisten with brandy or rum and form the mixture into a ball. Then cover with marzipan and sugarpaste (remember that some people are allergic to nuts or nut products).

To feed a rich fruit cake, peel away the base paper and brush on the soaking mixture. This way it will soak right into your cake. If you brush the top it will only soak the crust. Do not pierce the cake with a needle or skewer as this can result in the introduction of mould into the cake.

To soak a cake use one part brandy, one part rum and one part glycerine mixed together. Brush this over the base of the cake every few days.

When making royal icing all the equipment must be completely grease free. Wash the bowl/beater/spoon in very hot water and leave to dry before using. If making small amounts by hand then keep a wooden spoon specifically for this purpose and don't use it to beat cake mixtures as wood is porous and can retain fat.

Use white vegetable fat to grease your tins with as vegetable oil may burn. It is easy to wipe off after baking with kitchen paper.

To attach ribbon to a cake place in water, remove and pull through your fingers to remove the excess water. Place around the cake and hold the ends in place with a large pin (remove this when the ribbon is dry).

Patterns

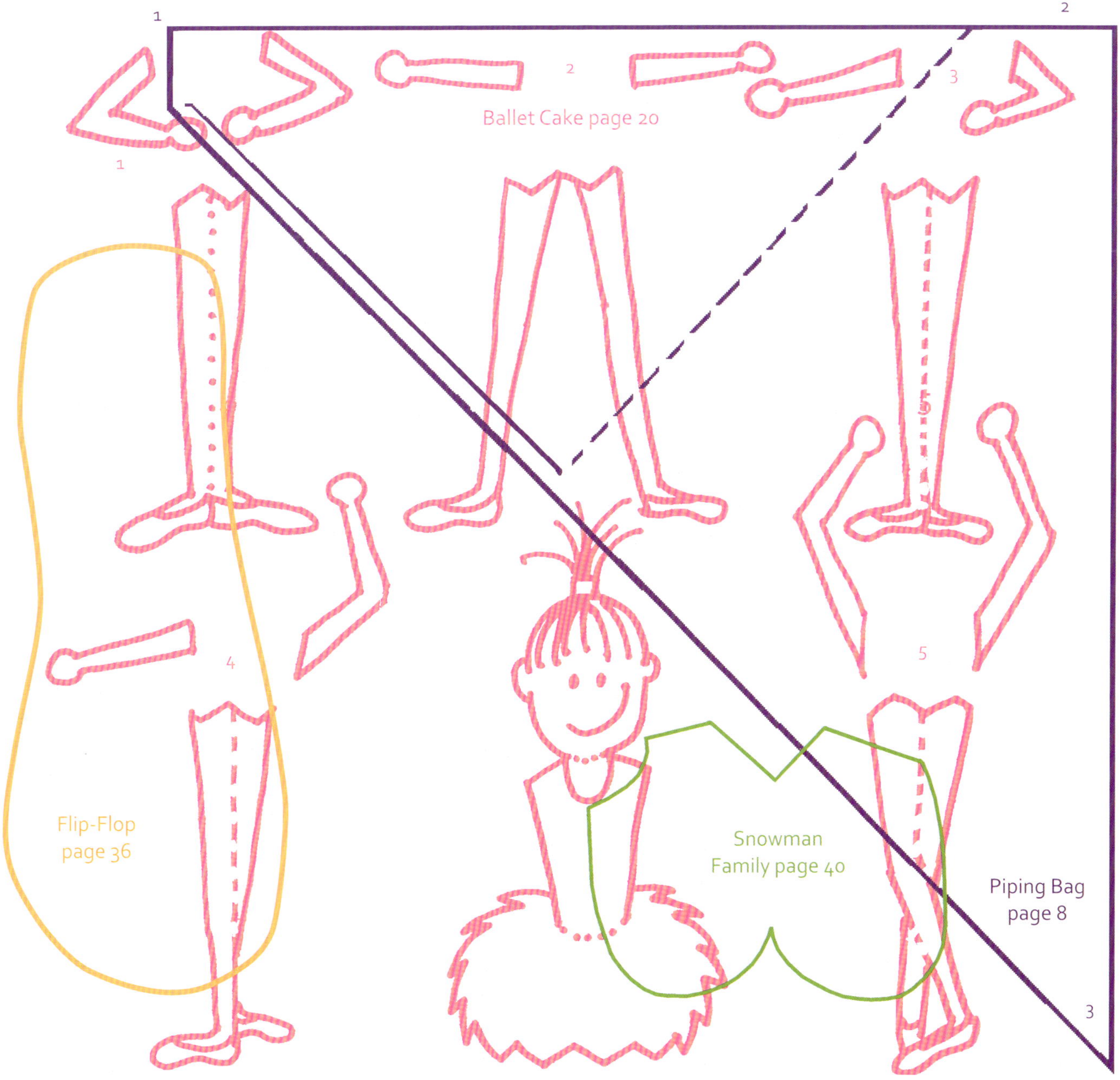
1
2
2
3
Ballet Cake page 20
1
4
5
Flip-Flop
page 36
Snowman
Family page 40
Piping Bag
page 8
3

Index